GNIT

BOOKS BY WILL ENO
AVAILABLE FROM TCG

The Flu Season and Other Plays

ALSO INCLUDES:

Intermission
Tragedy: a tragedy

Gnit

Middletown

The Realistic Joneses (forthcoming)

Thom Pain (based on nothing)

GNIT

a fairly rough translation of
Henrik Ibsen's *Peer Gynt*

Will Eno

THEATRE COMMUNICATIONS GROUP
NEW YORK
2014

Gnit is published by Theatre Communications Group, Inc., 520 Eighth Avenue, 24th Floor, New York, NY 10018-4156

Gnit is published in arrangement with Oberon Books Ltd, 521 Caledonian Road, London, N7 9RH.

This publication is made possible in part by the New York State Council on the Arts with the support of Governor Andrew Cuomo and the New York State Legislature.

TCG books are exclusively distributed to the book trade by Consortium Book Sales and Distribution.

A catalogue record for this book is available from the Library of Congress.

ISBN 978-1-55936-477-5 (paperback)
ISBN 978-1-55936-789-9 (ebook)

First Edition, June 2014

Characters

Double-cast roles are in parentheses. This suggested configuration will require a number of quick-changes, but these are certainly in the spirit of the play.

MOTHER (UNCLE JOE, BEGGAR)

PETER

STRANGER 1, MALE (STRANGER 3, MOYNIHAN, VOICE, HUNTER, ROBBER, (voice of) SPHINX, SHACKLETON, PALE MAN, REPORTER)

STRANGER 2, FEMALE (BRIDESMAID, BRIDE, GROUPIE, WOMAN IN GREEN, HELEN, CASE WORKER, ANITRA, PASTOR, BREMER, ANNA)

TOWN (THE GREEN FAMILY, INTERNATIONAL MAN, BEGRIFFIN)

SOLVAY (BARTENDER, DARK LADY, GRAVEDIGGER, AUCTIONEER)

Gnit was first performed on 15 March 2013 at the Actors Theatre of Louisville by special arrangement with Signature Theatre and United Talent Agency, with the following cast (in order of appearance):

MOTHER	Linda Kimbrough
PETER	Dan Waller
STRANGER 1	Kris Kling
STRANGER 2	Kate Eastwood Norris
TOWN	Danny Wolohan
SOLVAY	Hannah Bos

Various locations, various times.

Director	Les Waters
Scenic Designer	Antje Ellermann
Costume Designer	Connie Furr-Soloman
Lighting Designer	Matt Frey
Sound Designer	Bray Poor
Stage Manager	Paul Mills Holmes
Assistant Stage Manager	Lizzy Lee
Dramaturg	Amy Wegener
Casting	Stephanie Klapper

Director underwritten by Todd P. Lowe and Fran C. Ratterman; Bruce Merrick and Karen McCoy.

Gnit was developed at The Pershing Square Signature Center, with thanks to the JAW Festival, Portland Center Stage.

ACT FIRST

SCENE FIRST

The GNIT home (pronounced "Guh-nit"). Lights up on MOTHER, alone, in bed, recovering from a hysterectomy. Any movements she makes, throughout the scene, are made with a little difficulty.

MOTHER: Never have children. Or, I don't know, have children. You end up talking to yourself, either way.

Pause. PETER enters, with a small box.

PETER: Hi, Mom.

MOTHER: You're a liar.

PETER: That's a nice "welcome home."

MOTHER: No, it isn't.

PETER: God, Mom. I was trying to –

MOTHER: *(Interrupting.)* Yes, I'm sure you were. *(Noticing the small box that PETER holds.)* Is that for me?

PETER: What, this? Uh, yeah. You might not like it.

MOTHER: *(She opens it. It's a men's tie, yellow-green.)* You know, just because I can't have children anymore, because I don't have the organs for it anymore, doesn't mean I suddenly started goddamn wearing goddamn ties. Oh, but we're in luck. It's your color.

PETER: If you don't want it, I'll give it a try. *(Begins putting it on.)*

MOTHER: How kind.

PETER: Hey, it fits.

MOTHER: Aren't you even going to ask how I am?

PETER: How are you?

MOTHER: You promised you'd be here. What a darling boy. You lied.

PETER: I said I was sorry.

MOTHER: No, in fact, you didn't.

PETER: Well, I am.

MOTHER: No, in fact, you aren't.

PETER: Why don't you ever believe me?

MOTHER: Probably because you're always lying.

PETER: I was trying to tell you, if you'd just let me –

MOTHER: *(Interrupting.)* And because, when you begin
sentences with "I," I'm not even sure you know who you're
talking about. Because maybe I didn't hold you enough
when you were little.

PETER: You held me a lot.

MOTHER: I held you all the time. I never let you go. You were
very holdable. I held you and told you little stories to cover
up the sound of your father piddling our futures away.
(Pause.) I needed you, Peter. I was scared.

PETER: I'm sorry, mom.

MOTHER: I know you are, sweetheart. You always were.

PETER: I was trying to get home and then the –

MOTHER: *(Interrupting.)* Maybe if I'd let you babble more
when you were a baby, you wouldn't still be babbling now.

PETER: I'm not babbling, this is the story of –

MOTHER: *(Interrupting.)* "Mrs. Gnit, will someone be coming
to help you home?" "My son should be here any minute. I
think he's going to surprise me. I'll just wait here." And we
all stared down a long empty hallway. Surprise!

PETER: I was trying to –

MOTHER: *(Interrupting.)* Just be quiet.

PETER: So now I can't even open my mouth?

MOTHER: That's all you can do. Like a little fuzzy baby bird.
Making little peeps for its dirty worm.

PETER: *(Pause.)* Peep peep. *(Brief pause.)* Is there any chance I could get that dirty worm now? *(Brief pause.)* I like your dress.

MOTHER: I'm glad you're home, you big old disappointment.

PETER: *(Wanting to tell a story.)* I almost didn't make it.

MOTHER: *(Not wanting to hear it.)* But you did. Where's the cat?

PETER: Probably outside.

MOTHER: Can you get me the blanket? I think it's under the bed.

PETER: *(He starts looking for the blanket, which isn't under the bed.)* So, yeah, no, I almost didn't make it.

MOTHER: There's supposed to be a frost tonight.

PETER: Huh. Anyway, so a few days ago, I'm looking around, and what do I see, but a –

MOTHER: *(Interrupting.)* It isn't under the bed?

PETER: No. What do I see, but this crazy dog. Wild, but familiar; brown fur, but with Dad's eyes. So I took off after it.

MOTHER: Okay.

PETER: What?

MOTHER: No, go ahead.

PETER: I will. So, I could so easily see the thing, shivering on a rusty tangled chain, while a family dined inside, in silence. There it sits, banished – hungry and getting smarter. Scrawniness is power, it seemed to say. I wanted to know its secret.

MOTHER: I don't think dogs have secrets. *(Admiring her dress.)* Do you really like this dress?

PETER: It's fine. Yeah, so this dog. I started screaming my own name, chasing after it. God. Wow. *(He stares off, dreamily.)*

MOTHER: *(Brief pause.)* And? I'm not interested – but, don't leave us hanging. Did you catch it?

PETER: Yes and no. We ran through backyards, boy and dog, together. My legs got all scratched up. Somebody shot at us, I think.

MOTHER: *(Concerned.)* No.

PETER: Yeah. I think. People screamed. I didn't recognize anything. The dog, now limping, now half-wearing a pretty dress from a clothesline we'd run though, and me. Man and Nature, Mom. On a journey without maps, through a new theology, bible-less. And I suddenly could see that the –

MOTHER: *(Interrupting.)* God, what is that smell? Do you smell that? Oh, God, it's terrible.

PETER: I don't smell anything. But, so there we were. I saw the world as if I'd just turned a corner onto it. This was my moment. I wanted to –

MOTHER: *(Still trying to find the source of the smell.)* Is it your shoes? Did you step in something?

PETER: *(He sniffs his shoes and is repulsed.)* Oh, God. Yeah, I did. Sorry. Fuck.

MOTHER: Take them off, Peter. Get them outside. And don't swear. *(He exits.)* Love is in the air. *(PETER returns with his shoes off.)* Light a candle or some matches. *(Brief pause.)* We don't have any candles. Maybe I hung that blanket up outside.

PETER: So, the dog and I. It had been a few days now and the hunger and blood loss were getting us somewhere special. I was seeing stars. I don't know what the dog was seeing. Sticks? Bones? Stars, just like me? I don't know, I'm not a veterinarian. We stopped to breathe and I was rubbing my leg and then the dog just bolted. Then I looked up, and, there was the house, and, here I was, Home.

MOTHER: Really?

PETER: Really, Mom. Mom, I never felt so alive.

MOTHER: No? Not even last year? When the exact same thing happened? And you couldn't get home in time to take me in for my tests? You told me the exact same story, last year.

PETER: What do you mean, last–. No, come on– I felt alive then, too. This was different. This time, at first, I was thinking –

MOTHER: *(Interrupting.)* Enough, Peter. I can't, okay. No more. *(Brief pause.)* God, I can't get warm.

PETER: Here. *(He puts his jacket over her.)*

MOTHER: Can you tell me what you were born for? Honestly? Because I can't.

PETER: Well, you always told me –

MOTHER: *(Interrupting.)* I'm sure I told you something. *(Finds a little bag of candies in PETER's jacket pocket.)* What are these?

PETER: Oh, yeah, I forgot. I thought you used to like those.

MOTHER: Yes, I did, Pee-Wee. I did used to like these. *(She tries one.)* You're a good boy, Peter. You're like your father.

PETER: You hated dad.

MOTHER: I *disliked* your father, and was deeply offended by him. I never hated him. You be careful or you'll end up just like him.

PETER: Oh, no. I've got bigger plans.

MOTHER: So did he.

PETER: I'm on a journey to discover, to uncover, the authentic self.

MOTHER: Yeah? Get some milk, while you're out. *(Brief pause.)* I'm sorry about what I said, Peter. You were born because I needed you. Let me see your legs.

PETER: *(PETER rolls up his torn pants.)* Dueling scars, from my run-in with the world.

MOTHER: Cuts on your legs from running in the woods like an idiot.

PETER: Well, potayto, potahto.

MOTHER: There's rubbing alcohol in there. *(Pointing to a cabinet. PETER gets the rubbing alcohol. MOTHER prepares to put it on PETER's cuts.)* That girl should be doing this. That girl you used to skate with.

PETER: Sarah.

MOTHER: I think she still loves you. With her brains and looks and her money, and your – all your wonderful things, your posture – what children you'd have. You could do worse than marrying her. Just think. We could get new windows.

PETER: Maybe I should. She's pretty. *(He winces, due to the sting of the alcohol being applied.)* Jesus. I should give that a go. I liked her. I should. Christ. She'd make me happy and calm. I could find myself. God, Fuck, that stings. She loved me. I should marry her. Auugh! Fucking Jesus Shit! I will. I'll marry her.

MOTHER: She's getting married this afternoon. I'm sorry, Peter. I don't know why I even brought it up. Probably some unconscious thing.

PETER: *(Very calmly, softly.)* Fucking Jesus Shit.

MOTHER: Don't swear, Peter.

PETER: Sarah's getting married.

MOTHER: Maybe if you'd worked harder at school or been born a different person...who knows?

PETER: Yeah, that's true, actually. *(Brief pause.)* You know what, I'm going to the wedding. I'll just show up. I'll have her, and with her idiot father's idiot consent. I always respected him. This just somehow feels right.

MOTHER: No it doesn't. This feels stupid and wrong. Just forget it, please. I just got out of the hospital. I need you here.

PETER: *(He wasn't listening.)* I'll need to leave, right away. And I'll need you to come with me. Talk me up, a little, with the in-laws. The Gnits will rise again!

MOTHER: No, we won't.

PETER: Yes, they will.

MOTHER: Peter, please – I just need to eat some protein.

PETER: Ah, I love you, ma. I should put you up on the roof or something.

MOTHER: That doesn't make any sense.

PETER: Doesn't it?

MOTHER: No. Did you even hear one word I just said?

PETER: Yeah. Definitely. "Children." And, I think, "posture," a while ago. So there's two – you only asked for one. Listen, I know this seems hectic. I know I seem a little hectic, right now. But I know it's right. This is the moment. I thought it was that dog, but, no. This'll be the moment. When my whole life, everything, changed. I promise. I'm the man of the house, now. I'll take care of you. I will. I'll comfort you, mother. *(Motioning toward jacket.)* Could I grab my, yeah, there we go – *(PETER takes his jacket back, gently.)* Wait, so who's she marrying?

MOTHER: That Moynihan. Come here, dear. Your collar is wrong.

PETER: Moynihan? I think I'd make a much better person than Moyniha – *(PETER has moved towards her bedside. MOTHER violently grabs PETER by the collar or tie.)*

MOTHER: *(Interrupting.)* You're killing me, Peter. I'm so tired of the cold. I'm tired of the free church food. So go ahead, you go and try to get yourself married to that girl. Because, you know what? We need help. We're poor. Did you know that? We're poor people. I have a condition. We have broken windows and medical bills. We're in trouble. And you are killing your dying mother. *(She lets PETER go.)*

PETER: I understand.

MOTHER: No, you don't.

PETER: Well, who's to say.

MOTHER: Be careful, Peter. Don't go die some ridiculous death.

PETER: I will, Mom. Thanks. I won't be long. Bye.

MOTHER: I really need you here. I need you. So come back home, soon, okay.

PETER: Definitely.

MOTHER: What did I just say?

PETER: *(He was not paying attention.)* Oh. Just, that when, or, I shouldn't, you said I shouldn't feel that I need –

MOTHER: Get out of here, Peter. *(PETER exits. MOTHER eats another piece of candy.)* Sometimes, it's like I'm still pregnant with him. I mean, sometimes, I still get a little kick out of him.

SCENE SECOND

PETER enters, on his way to the wedding. Two strangers approach. PETER has hidden.

STRANGER 1: Oh, my god, yeah – half drunk half the time, just sort of stupid the rest. He's just, "Me, me, me." I mean, that's him, saying that. I heard that one time he actually –

PETER: *(He steps out of bush. Pointedly.)* Sorry to interrupt. I suppose you're talking about me?

STRANGER 1: Ah, no – sorry, buddy. *(He turns to continue talking to STRANGER 2.)* He's terrible with old people, unkind to animals. *(He turns back to PETER.)* Hey, wait a minute – you're Peter Gnit, aren't you. You're actually just like the guy I was just talking about. *(To STRANGER 2.)* In fact, he's probably worse.

STRANGER 2: What smells like urine?

PETER: Is this a quiz?

STRANGER 2: No. I smell urine.

PETER: Well, don't look at me.

STRANGER 1: We're both staring directly at you. *(STRANGER 1 and 2 begin to walk away.)* Anyway, as I was saying, this other guy was such a jerk, such a liar. But at least he didn't have any pride about it. That's what makes Gnit so much worse. He actually has the temerity to think he's got something to offer us all.

STRANGER 2: Is temerity like recklessness?

STRANGER 1: Sort of, yeah.

STRANGER 2: That's what I thought.

STRANGER 1: Vocabulary.

STRANGER 2: Yeah. *(Very brief pause.)* I guess in our relationship, you're the one who talks more.

STRANGER 1: *(Modestly.)* Oh, I don't know about that, but, thank you. *(They both exit.)*

PETER: *(He tries to smell his underarm.)* I'm not a – whatever he said. I'm not. Let's see. I need a plan, here. *(Brief pause.)* That cloud looks like a cloud. That cloud looks like me, kind of. I am, in my eyes, the King of the Clouds.

STRANGER 3: *(Enters.)* Hi, I'm a person. Now, I doubt you're with the wedding, dressed like you are, smelling like you do. Are you? If so, the path to the wedding is that-a-way. If not, the path off my property is this-a-way. So, now, I've offered you a couple of different courses of action, a couple different a-ways off my land. Don't make me do something I don't want to do. Which I would very happily do.

PETER: Do you know who I am?

STRANGER 3: Yes, I do. Actually, let me be honest, here – no, I don't. I'm sure you're someone. Get off my property. *(Brief pause. He opens his arms, in a gesture that seems to say, "I told you to leave, what are you still doing here?" PETER mimics the gesture. STRANGER 3 points off-stage. PETER mimics this, too.)* Stop imitating me.

PETER: I'm not imitating you. You're just doing it sooner. *(PETER exits. STRANGER 3 exits.)*

SCENE THIRD

At the wedding.

TOWN: *(Enters, a single person.)* Some nights I get so drunk
I think I'm a whole fucking town. I get liquored up into
such a state, into so many states, that I feel as angry and
judgmental and beautiful as a whole town. Whole town.
I shouldn't have smoked that cigar. *(PETER enters, other
side of the stage.)* Hey, look – it's that Peter Gnit. What's he
doing here? No, don't look, don't look. Great, he's coming
over here. Hey, watch it, you almost spilled on my jacket.
Yeah, I'll fucking smash this glass right into your eye. Guys,
guys, guys. *(Brief pause.)* The bride seems really moody.
She really loves Moynihan, though. You can tell. *(PETER
approaches.)* Hey, the entertainment is here. Gnit, tell us
a story. Here's some booze, monkey-man. *(TOWN hands
PETER a bottle.)*

PETER: I thank you, sir. Not a monkey, though. *(PETER clears
his throat.)* Let's see. *(PETER drinks.)* A child was born one
Monday or the year before, on a Tuesday. All sorts of
forces assembled against him – even the shape of his head
was determined by outside pressure. Nonetheless, if that's
a word, feeling himself an emperor, somehow, he left to
somehow found his empire. *(A quick sip.)* This is good.
What is this? *(He takes a quick look at the label.)* Lingonberry
– that's interesting. Anyway, he went through rain and sun
and snow, unto himself, as life's many doors and trapdoors
opened before him. End of story, basically. Many years
later, in a private ceremony, he was crowned the Subject
of Subjects and lowered into the final earth. *(Glances at the
label again.)* You know, I bet this would go really well with
another bottle of this.

TOWN: Huh. Not a bad tale. Really? That was the only bottle.
So, the main guy died – did not see that coming. Sorry,
where did they have cigars? You look stupid because
you're poor and I'm going to punch you in the face. Hey,
whoa – those are fightin' words. People, again, please, this
is a wedding feast. This town is driving me crazy. *(PETER*

has drifted away.) Hey, look, Gnit is up to something over there. Where? Right there. Oh yeah.

PETER approaches BRIDESMAID. Music playing at a low level.

PETER: Let me introduce the real me. Hi.

BRIDESMAID: Who invited you?

PETER: I did.

BRIDESMAID: Well then I think you should ask yourself to leave.

PETER: Do you want to fuck around? You know, weather permitting?

BRIDESMAID: That is so rude.

PETER: But is it really, though?

BRIDESMAID: Yes. *(Calling off-stage.)* Richard, this guy was just really rude to me. *(Exits.)*

PETER: *(SOLVAY enters.)* I think she misconstrued what I said.

SOLVAY: Hello.

PETER: Hi.

SOLVAY: My name is Solvay.

PETER: What a coincidence.

SOLVAY: How is it a coincidence?

PETER: No, just, great name. "Solvay." It makes me want to ask for forgiveness. You know, "Atone, atone."

SOLVAY: I never had that reaction to it. I'm, um...

PETER: What?

SOLVAY: Nothing.

PETER: Did you want to, would you care to join –

SOLVAY: *(Interrupting.)* I'm fine. I love this song. *(Looks at TOWN, who sips a drink, maybe dances a few small dance steps.)* Look at everybody. It's quite a crowd. *(TOWN waves a small awkward wave.)*

PETER: It's a good crowd.

SOLVAY: Are you here with the –

PETER: *(Interrupting.)* My name's Peter Gnit.

SOLVAY: "Gnit?" I've heard about you. *(Brief pause.)* I've always wondered about that name – where's it from?

PETER: It's a typo.

SOLVAY: Oh.

PETER: Yeah, some mix-up from a birth certificate but we just decided to go with it. Will you have this dance with me?

SOLVAY: I've heard about you, I said.

PETER: Come on. Dance with me. What are you afraid of?

SOLVAY: Nothing. I don't know. My father. The town. My body, and disease. Heights, small spaces, drowning, you, poverty. *(A little laugh.)* I'm not afraid of anything. Except loneliness, choking, stroke, drowning, anything socially-transmitted, the dark, weakness, guilt, this, you, I don't know, loneliness, going blind, history, this, things like this, my father, fathers.

PETER: Right, but I mean – actually, yeah, wow, that's a pretty good list. Drowning – ouch.

SOLVAY: I have to go.

PETER: No you don't. Stay.

SOLVAY: Why?

PETER: There's something here. Between us. A moment, maybe. A long moment.

SOLVAY: Did you hear all the things I'm afraid of?

PETER: Yeah.

SOLVAY: And you're not scared?

PETER: No, I'm scared.

SOLVAY: That makes me feel good.

PETER: Did you ever just want to feel – I don't even know how to say it – welcomed, in life? Just, give me a smile, world.

Like I'm not in the wrong place. Just soup and a blanket, and everything's all right. Did you ever want that?

SOLVAY: Yes. *(Brief pause.)* Soup and a blanket. You're very... I don't know. I'll just say that: You're very.

PETER: Thank you.

SOLVAY: You're welcome. *(Brief pause.)* I have to go. *(She exits.)*

PETER: I like your worldview.

MOYNIHAN: *(Enters.)* Jesus, Jesus, Jesus – fuck.

PETER: *(To himself.)* Solvay.

MOYNIHAN: My wife-to-be won't come out of the bathroom.

PETER: Your wife-to-be or not-to-be? Do you remember your Shakespeare? Not me. See, mainly, I'm a people person, in the executive mold, with good problem-causing skills.

TOWN drifts nearby, stands downstage.

MOYNIHAN: I didn't know that. But, so, she won't come out of the bathroom. I don't know what I said. Maybe you could talk to her?

PETER: Sure. *(PETER turns, moves a little downstage, toward TOWN, strikes a soliloquist's pose. Speaks to TOWN, and somewhat toward the audience.)* And here the villain seeks your complicity. I do this for the benefit of my mother, for Family with a large F, and for the benefit of those who like to cry at weddings.

TOWN: Sorry, is that, are you saying that to me? Yeah, what was that? It's like he said this whole weird thing. Are we supposed to say anything back?

PETER: No, you don't have to say anything.

TOWN: Okay. Do you know... did you guys happen to know, that this whole function hall was once an old candle factory? Interesting. That wasn't interesting. Well, it wasn't uninteresting. Yes, it was. No, it wasn't.

PETER: Are you done?

TOWN: Hi.

PETER: Hi. *(To MOYNIHAN.)* Let me see what I can do, okay? That is the question.

MOYNIHAN: Thanks. *(PETER moves upstage.)* They used to skate together.

TOWN: *(Awkward pause. To MOYNIHAN.)* Big day, huh? Yeah, it's like: I sentence you to a sentence with life in, like, here's your ball and chain, hello?, life sentence, watch out. *(Very brief pause.)* That didn't come out right. No, it didn't. He's been drinking. We've all been drinking. But, so, yeah, congratulations. Yeah, congrats.

MOYNIHAN: Thanks. God, I'm a nervous wreck.

MOYNIHAN is downstage, facing audience, while PETER quietly jimmies open the bathroom door, disappears inside, returns with BRIDE over his shoulder and sneaks off. TOWN exits, to have a look.

UNCLE JOE: *(Enters.)* You should probably hear about this. Gnit just ran off with your wife over his shoulder. Or, I guess, fiancé. It happened about, I would say, ten to fifteen feet behind you.

MOYNIHAN: What? Are you serious? Where were they go –

UNCLE JOE: *(Interrupting.)* When do we eat, Paul? Hunger is all I remember from any wedding I've ever been to. Hunger and waiting. And then, finally, a cold plate of bad food. At least at funerals they get you in and out.

TOWN: *(Enters.)* Gnit made off with the unhappy bride! Wasn't her dress amazing? The unhappy bride was laughing and waving! The whole town just stood there. The pig! I'm so drunk, right now. What was that fabric? Let's kill him! Revenge! Tablecloths always make me sad – isn't that weird? I said fucking Revenge.

MOYNIHAN: I think I'm going to be sick.

UNCLE JOE: Is there any crackers or anything around here, Paul? I'm going to see if I can find some crackers. *(Exits.)*

MOYNIHAN: What am I going to do?

TOWN: He humiliated all of us. Me, most of all. I'm the girl's father. He is. And I swear to you all, I am going to kill him, and you will swear along with me that it was an accident. Now, let's go! Wait a minute – if she's so unhappy, why would she laugh? Shut up, Richard. Yeah, this is no time to think. Hey, your tie's all crooked, here, let me get that. *(TOWN straightens his collar.)* Much better. So, Marek was just telling everyone about how this place used to be some kind of an old candle fac – . I said, let's fucking go. Factory. An old candle factory.

MOTHER: *(Enters, moving with difficulty.)* What's going on? What happened? Don't tell me. No, tell me. Is the wedding over?

TOWN: Sort of.

MOYNIHAN: That's all you have to say? *(TOWN shrugs.)* The little liar ran off with her. Gnit, I'm talking about. He kidnapped her. We were going to be happy. That was the plan. I did the seating.

MOTHER: What does the girl's father think?

MOYNIHAN: He's going to shoot Gnit in the back and get one of these upstanding townspeople here to lie and say it was an accident.

MOTHER: You're not serious.

TOWN: We are. We just suddenly changed, from a little group standing around, to a bloodthirsty mob on a mission. Don't worry, ma'am, just let me assure you he'll be dead or in serious pain by morning.

MOTHER: He's my son.

TOWN: Oh. We didn't know that. *(Very brief pause.)* I did – Hi, Mrs. Gnit. Sorry. I thought you were a caterer or something. Let's go. Time is wasting. My anger is wasting. The mob has spoken.

MOYNIHAN: Someone has to die, for all the dead things inside me.

TOWN: *(Finding the above philosophically distasteful.)* Ewww.

MOYNIHAN: What?

TOWN: No, nothing, that was great. Let's go. He's getting away. *(Begins to exit.)*

MOTHER: Please wait. Good townspeople...

TOWN: You have one minute. Yeah, because, we really should... Yeah.

MOTHER: Please listen. People get struck by lightning, playing golf. They drown, skinny-dipping, drunk. We get skin cancer, lying in the sun at the beach. All very silly, in the end, the way of all flesh. The best of all is to die in the night, at home, quietly, just from having not died for so long. Let my son die a silly natural death. Just let him suffer the normal humiliations. Don't hurt him. I'm the boy's mother. Please. I'm asking you.

TOWN: Well, we're the boy's lynch mob and we're telling you. No, hang on, those were good points. I think I speak for all of us when I say we're a little torn. Let's go. But, wait, if we actually picture the moment of the hammer hitting the head, or the screwdriver entering the ear – I said, Let's go. You know, Richard, I don't think you should come. No, he should come. It should be everyone. We speak with one voice. Bye. Don't run. Yeah, let's pace ourselves. *(TOWN exits.)*

MOTHER: Cartoons. You're all just thoughtless cruel cartoons. And so am I. And how do you draw a drawing of me to show what I'm feeling? How do you spell the sound of an old lady being hit in the stomach with the facts of her life? Not "pow." Or "wham." It's quieter than that. It's smaller and almost all vowels. The sound of an old woman, being hurt. Or the sound of a son, not turning out like anyone wanted. It's just a little sound. God. Ohhh.

ACT SECOND

SCENE FIRST

BRIDE and PETER. In the mountains.

BRIDE: You should've seen their faces how I saw their faces, upside-down, and so mad. Yelling, "Kill him. Kill the lucky vermin." With my former husband-to-be at the front, his new tuxedo all torn up, and tears in his eyes. Then the screams turned to wheezing and all I could hear was you breathing.

PETER: It was really something, wasn't it.

BRIDE: I was hoping you'd save me. Maybe I was just scared, but, I think I was making a big mistake.

PETER: Yeah. Listen, maybe you following me here wasn't the best idea.

BRIDE: You carried me here.

PETER: Yeah, I know. Hey, so who was Solvay? Was she with you or the groom or what?

BRIDE: Who? Should we make a fire?

PETER: I think we'll be all right. *(Brief pause.)* I'm in love.

BRIDE: I'm in love, too.

PETER: It's an amazing feeling, isn't it. *(Brief pause.)* So, yeah, are we clear?

BRIDE: What?

PETER: You should go back down, okay? You can probably still catch the end of the, you know, your wedding. I thought that other moment was the moment, the one with the dog, or running off with you, but now I have a better grasp on things. This is it. Solvay is.

BRIDE: Don't even joke, Peter.

PETER: Okay.

BRIDE: I have nowhere to go back down to. I gave up everything for you. My father's love, security, money, Moynihan. I ruined my life for you.

PETER: Thanks, I guess. But, as I said, you know – well, I already said it.

BRIDE: Are you – . Peter? I can't believe you're doing this. What about all the things you said? And all the times we –

PETER: *(Interrupting.)* I was probably drunk, okay? I can see how this could look ugly. But, what can I do – I gotta be me.

BRIDE: Do you? *(Brief pause.)* You ruined my life.

PETER: Yeah, you said. And I said I was sorry. On second thought, you were with me every step of the way.

BRIDE: You had me in a headlock, you fucking – . Do you even –

PETER: *(He interrupts.)* Sshhh. That's enough. Go away. I'm all sobered up, now. Isn't this awful. For whatever reason, I don't even want to bother coming up with something final to say. Death to your memory. That's actually pretty final.

BRIDE: Someday, if you're lucky, you'll look back and it will hurt you to think about this. You hurt someone who, admittedly, had a lot of problems, but who was still just a person who loved you.

PETER: Okay, very good.

BRIDE: *(Simply, plainly.)* Oh my God. I'm having a panic attack. Thank you so much. I'm in the woods in a wedding dress, on my wedding day, having a panic attack. *(She exits.)*

PETER: Panic attack. That can't feel good. It's probably just cold feet. *(He strolls off.)*

SCENE SECOND

In the mountains. MOTHER and SOLVAY.

MOTHER: I just need to sit for a bit.

SOLVAY: We'll find him. He has to be somewhere.

MOTHER: I keep seeing him, dead and broken, lying backwards in a ditch, animals gnawing on his muddy crotch. Mothers just have a sense.

SOLVAY: I have a feeling too.

MOTHER: That's nice.

SOLVAY: It really is. *(Very brief pause.)* I think he's wonderful. So full of life, and himself. He scared me. Then I liked him. He'll be okay.

MOTHER: It was good of you to come with me. People don't really help much. That's not true – people can be sweet.

SOLVAY: No, of course. I saw the whole town heading off, practically with rakes and torches. He doesn't deserve to get hurt. People don't understand him. I probably don't either, but, hurting him probably isn't going to help. Maybe I feel guilty about something, and, somehow, that explains something about me? I don't know.

MOTHER: Maybe. *(Brief pause.)* He used to come up here when he was little. I followed him once. He made a little clearing. He gathered all these little things together, some cloth and stones, an oak leaf. And he was talking to it all. He told the cloth, "You're a bad piece of cloth, because you're not a stone." And he told the stone it was disappointing it wasn't a leaf. And he had an animal bone he held up and said, "I don't even know where to start, with you." And then he said, "We're all the wrong thing. But here we are, together." And he sat there. Peter could be so quiet. I watched him till sunset. Then he put everything in a pile and said, "Bye, cloth. Goodbye, leafy. Bye, bone. I love you."

SOLVAY: Aww, that's a long story. "Goodbye, leafy." The poor thing. I used to make dolls, too.

MOTHER: We're not terrible people. I'm not a terrible mother.

SOLVAY: I know.

MOTHER: I think you'd make a wonderful person for Pee-Wee.

25

SOLVAY: *(She laughs.)* Ohh. "Pee-Wee." I think we'd be very happy. I don't know how I'm supposed to know this. But how do you know anything? Did you ever hear anyone say, "This is the moment. This is what I believe, now." And that was it and they made that their life, right then and there, forever and ever, and never looked back.

MOTHER: I have heard people say that. But they never followed through, or they got syphilis or something and then just disappeared. *(Very brief pause.)* But I'm sure it happens.

SOLVAY: That's what it was like for me. And it never was like that, before. I don't know what this feeling is, or where it came from, but I feel really sure about it.

MOTHER: And why is that, dear?

SOLVAY: No, I just said, it's not something I can really articulate.

MOTHER: No, of course. Men can be very attractive.

SOLVAY: Yeah, I know that, but, this is different.

MOTHER: I understand. Peter's father was a complete idiot.

SOLVAY: Is that, that's how you're showing you understand?

MOTHER: You're very sweet, dear.

SOLVAY: Let's just keep looking. *(MOTHER stops.)* Are you okay?

MOTHER: I just got out of the hospital. *(Brief pause.)* I'm amazed the world's children don't all die of guilt for the things they put the world's mothers through. *(Brief pause.)* You're very kind to care about us.

SOLVAY: Of course. I do care about you, Mrs. Gnit.

MOTHER: Oh, you don't have to call me that, dear. Wait! *(She freezes, turns her head slightly sideways, listening.)*

SOLVAY: *(Pause. They both listen.)* Did you hear something?

MOTHER: I thought I did. I'm a mother, you know – we have a sense. Although, sometimes, it's wrong. *(They exit.)*

SCENE THIRD

The mountains.

PETER: *(Enters.)* "Tall peaks in the distance. Late day, the shadows lengthen. Amid wild mountain flowers and babbling brooks, a solitary figure approaches." That's a stage direction from some play I read in school. Probably should have paid more attention. Or not, or not. *(Brief pause.)* Maybe I should go back and face the whole music and just get it over with. Start my life with Solvay. It'd be good. Good food, the indoors, love, company, the true self. I'll go back.

GROUPIE: *(Enters.)* Hi.

PETER: Hello. Beautiful evening.

GROUPIE: Isn't it. God, it's gorgeous. It's great being outside.

PETER: It can be, yup. What brings you up here?

GROUPIE: We're from the city, my two girlfriends and I. We're groupies.

PETER: I see. Groupies following some bearded guru or a promising local act?

GROUPIE: No. Just groupies.

PETER: With no...yeah, I get it. Just groupies. *(With interest.)* Really? Maybe I could join you. Or you could join me.

GROUPIE: Yeah, I don't know. We're here mainly for the air. But, do you want to have a glass of wine with us? We're kind of in the mood to be crazy and also we're a little high.

PETER: Crazy is a watchword of mine. A little high is my philosophy. Your gracious offer I gladly accept. You picked the right mountaintop of the right range on the night of the right sunset.

GROUPIE: You're funny. Not funny ha-ha, but, like, funny redundant. Come on. We're over here. *(She motions off-stage. They exit.)*

TOWN: *(Enters, somewhat out of breath.)* Fucking. The fucking. Hey, slow down. You're not even winded. I want to see

27

that bastard writhe, blood in his ears and eyes. Yeah, I play tennis three times a week, just try to stay active. Why don't we just go home. Moynihan did. No! I think I got poison ivy. I want to sit down. No, we're not stopping till we're dripping red. *(Indecipherable grumbling.)* What? I didn't say anything. Make sure you don't touch your eye. Yeah, you should wash your hands. Hey, look at this, this is Bergfrue – also known as pyramidal saxifrage. It's a nice little flower. Are we stopping or what? Death! It's almost like a little daisy. *(TOWN exits.)*

PETER: *(Enters, with GROUPIE, speaking to another person off-stage.)* Please, why not, more champagne. The lamb was delicious.

GROUPIE: You're so authentic.

PETER: Yeah. I was really hungry. *(Begins to exit.)*

GROUPIE: Where are you going?

PETER: Now? Just going to find some more kindling.

GROUPIE: Oh. Okay.

PETER: Don't sigh. Your good man shall return. *(Aside.)* Like hell he will. Thanks for the so-so experience.

GROUPIE: "Like hell he will"? "Thanks for the so-so experience"?

PETER: Oh. *(Very brief pause.)* Sorry about that.

GROUPIE: You know, I teach art in prison and I have several advanced degrees in molecular – why am I even wasting my breath.

PETER: I don't know.

GROUPIE: You're just like everyone else. *(GROUPIE exits.)*

PETER: Me? No. That's probably the problem. I'm not enough like everyone else. *(He seems a little dazed.)* I'm wiped out. Let's see. I've got a big heart and I'm having palpitations. I could soliloquize, I could faint – lot of possibilities. *(He faints.)*

SCENE FOURTH

SOMEONE walks by, looks at the unconscious PETER for a while, gives him a little kick, looks around, then walks away. WOMAN IN GREEN enters. She puts cold water on PETER's forehead.

PETER: Are you a dream? Are you an angel?

WOMAN IN GREEN: If I were a dream or an angel, wouldn't I know all about that dog you chased and how it got all caught up in a woman's dress from a clothesline?

PETER: I guess. You still look like an angel.

WOMAN IN GREEN: You look like a person.

PETER: I try to be myself. Because, really, that's just a large part of who I am.

WOMAN IN GREEN: We don't get a lot of people around here. This is really mysterious. I've dreamed about someone like you. I sit in my room and I have dreams and I'm starting to think they're about you. Do you believe in fate? Or other explanations? *(She takes his hand and they exit.)*

TOWN: *(Enters.)* Are we – I think we're going in circles. It was good to get out of the house, but I think this is it for me. Let's stay out here, I like it out here. No, no, me too, I'm going back, too. We'll fuck up Gnit when he comes back home. The air really is n-n-nice out h-h-here. Who are you? You haven't said one word this whole time. I s-s-s-stutter. I th-th-th-thought you'd-d-d-d laugh. *(Short laugh.)* Hey, maybe we could fuck this guy up, instead? I mean, here he is, right here. True, we wouldn't have to go chasing him all over. Wh-wh-why would you duh-duh-do that? Let's bully this guy later – I'm famished. Y-y-you p-p-people are m-m-mean. Come on, guys. Make sure you bring your trash. Wh-wh-wh-wait for muh-muh-muh me. Okay, come on, slowpoke. S-s-slow-poke. I f-f-fucking like that. *(Exits.)*

PETER: *(Enters, with WOMAN IN GREEN. His rumpled clothing is even more rumpled.)* Well, that was, you know, that was very good. *(Very brief pause.)* God, is it morning, or is daytime just starting to look sadder? You know? Jesus.

WOMAN IN GREEN: Time is funny.

PETER: Yes, it is.

WOMAN IN GREEN: Here comes my family.

PETER: Where?

WOMAN IN GREEN: It'll just be another second. *(Very long pause.)* Here they are.

THE GREEN FAMILY: *(Enters, a single person.)* Hello.

PETER: Are there more of you?

THE GREEN FAMILY: I think this is everyone.

PETER: Well then hello. Good evening. Good day.

WOMAN IN GREEN: Daddy, everyone – this is Peter.

THE GREEN FAMILY: Hello. Hi. How's it going? We'll make this quick. We're in real estate. We need a son-in-law. And a brother-in-law. For reasons you don't need to know. You and our daughter seem to be sexually simpatico. You are he. Our new son. Hey, brother. Welcome aboard. You're very rich, now. Be nice or we'll operate on you, and we aren't really doctors. Now, a toast.

PETER: This is all very flattering.

THE GREEN FAMILY: Isn't it? I know, it's so flattering.

PETER: It really is. But I'm afraid I'll need a little time.

THE GREEN FAMILY: Take all the time you want. *(Very brief pause.)* Have you decided?

PETER: Good people, good woman, I must decline. Or, at least, defer.

WOMAN IN GREEN: What about over there, before, in the willow tree? You started yelling, and I said, "Don't finish inside me," but you did, anyway. And now I might be pregnant. What about all the things you yelled? I gave myself to you. So now please just do what any fox or marmoset or the other monogamous animal would do, and stay with me.

PETER: I'm afraid I can't.

THE GREEN FAMILY: We're afraid you must. Put on this suit. Here's a briefcase. *(Puts the suit jacket on him.)*

PETER: You're very insistent. You know what? Why not? Give me that. *(He grabs the briefcase. He's pleased with his new look.)* I could see this, maybe. Yeah. How's this sound? "Cancel my morning massage. Reschedule my afternoon massage. Listen, I've got a little place I'd buy myself but company policy forbids it. You really just got to see the place, owned by an old lady, never hurt a fly, used to cry herself to sleep, and she wants it to go to a decent sort, a sort like you, and like I say, I'd buy it myself, because I'm like you, but you're even more like you, so why don't we fill out some papers and put you in your new home, how do you like the sound of that, 'Your new home,' see, it's already, linguistically speaking, yours, so now all you got to do is buy it. Get me a pen, darling. Do you want a cup of coffee?" How was that?

THE GREEN FAMILY: Not bad. What did I tell you? You were born for this. If he was born for anything. That's enough, Steven. I was kidding – I'm sure he'll be fine. *(Whispering.)* Empty-headed fucking parrot.

PETER: Pardon?

THE GREEN FAMILY: Nothing. Yeah, I didn't hear anything. So, are we all right, here?

PETER: I have to say, it feels pretty good.

THE GREEN FAMILY: Does it. Our one rule around here, is, "By yourself, for yourself." Do it our way, and, things fall into place.

PETER: It's all I've ever done. This could really work out.

THE GREEN FAMILY: Here, dress it up with this pocket square. *(Puts a folded pocket square in PETER's breast pocket.)* Very nice. It brings out his eyes.

PETER: *(Brief pause.)* You know what? I can't. I'm sorry. Though I think that I – as a cloud-watching alcoholic – could probably do very well in a commission-driven industry, I really must say no. Good people, I am on a search, a search for the truest me. And I don't think I'll likely find him, here with you. Maybe I might, though.

THE GREEN FAMILY: Our daughter asked you nicely. So did we. So just say yes. And, just so you know, we'll gladly hear it, "Yes," as the last word you ever say, practically just a whisper, a last breath, trickling out of your bloody mouth, dirty newspaper stuck in the incisions made in your body by our unclean tools, following our failed operation. Steven, when did you get like this? Don't mind him. Hey, we're just crazy people. Or we're business people. Or just he is. Or, we're not.

PETER: I'm crazy too. I'd have to be to turn down your wonderful offer.

THE GREEN FAMILY: We asked you to be one of us. And you said no. It hurt. Now, we're going to hurt you back. Can we start, Dad? Yeah, kids – you go ahead. *(He nods, draws three knives out of his coat.)*

PETER: *(Pleading.)* Please, Sirs. I'm begging you –

THE GREEN FAMILY: We've seen begging before. And it hasn't made any difference. No, not true – remember the time we cut out a guy's mouth, instead of his eyes, because he wanted to see his kids grow up? Oh, yeah. Boy, we've done some awful things. But, we did them *together.* I always felt that, with the kids, it was important to always – *(They're interrupted by sirens, off-stage. THE GREEN FAMILY and WOMAN IN GREEN are frightened.)* Run! No, let's take him hostage! Him!? Are you kidding!? Let's go, just run! No. Just walk normally. *(They exit.)*

WOMAN IN GREEN: I love you. *(She makes quote marks with her fingers around the following word, although she says it earnestly.)* "Honestly." *(Exits.)*

SCENE FIFTH

Stage goes dark, but for PETER, in a cone of light. Sirens abruptly stop.
Amplified breathing.

PETER: Who is that? Who are you?

VOICE: Me.

PETER: Who's "me"?

VOICE: I am.

PETER: That's like something I'd say.

VOICE: Interesting.

PETER: I guess. So, who are you? Or, what are you?

VOICE: I'm the middle.

PETER: This is only the middle!?

VOICE: I'm the thing in-between things. The space between
spaces, the little lack of sound between words. Where the
air isn't going in or out. Call me peace, or, death. I'm what
you can't handle.

PETER: Maybe you want some of this! *(He throws a punch.)*

VOICE: I don't have a body. There's nothing to hit.

PETER: Then maybe you want some of this. *(He does nothing.)*

VOICE: Now you're talking.

PETER: How can I get past you?

VOICE: I'm not really anything, so it's impossible to get past
me. And I'm not actually real, so you'll never get over me.
Just try to live with me.

PETER: Is this philosophy?

VOICE: I don't know. Is *this* philosophy? *(A couple of breaths.)*

PETER: I don't know.

VOICE: Well, then I don't know either. See, I only exist in
correlation to your resistance to me. *(VOICE does not laugh.)*
Forgive me – I always have to laugh when I tell people
that.

PETER: How come you didn't laugh?

VOICE: It didn't seem funny, that time.

PETER: Wait a minute. I think I get it. Are you telling me I should just bide my time, just go with the flow? And then whatever's going to come to me will come to me? My reward in life?

VOICE: Yes.

PETER: But, is this true? And can you be trusted?

VOICE: No.

PETER: *(He tries to get past again. He can't.)* I give up.

VOICE: Me too.

PETER: *(Brief pause.)* So now what happens?

VOICE: We wait.

PETER: Okay. Not my favorite thing. *(Brief pause.)* I wonder if Solvay is waiting for me. That must be awful. Turning and listening, at every snapped twig. She probably feels completely alone. As if nobody cares and nobody loves her. As if I don't. *(He is a little choked up.)* Sort of surprised, by that feeling. Feeling bad for someone else. *(Brief pause.)* Hello? Thing? Middle? *(He looks around, something's changed and he's able to pass.)* Hey. How 'bout that.

SCENE SIXTH

Outside MOTHER's cabin. PETER is asleep, behind a bush.

A HUNTER with a gun enters and walks slowly across the stage.

HUNTER: Bleezie! *(Looking up.)* Hey, Grandpa – you up there? My poor dog has rabies. So I'm in the middle of a kind of sad adventure. I can't even imagine what I'm about to do. *(Very brief pause.)* My wife brought it home a bunch of years ago, the dog. The kids gave it this weird name that just sort of stuck. And, all of a sudden, Bleezie was with us all the time. Morning noon and night. My best friend of my life. *(Hears a sound from PETER's hiding place. Brief pause, listens.)* Anyway, so now here I am with a gun, trying to track her down, going to all her favorite spots, looking for a trail of foamy saliva, and wondering, if I can get a clear shot at my sick dog Bleezie-girl, will I be able to pull the trigger. *(Very brief pause.)* Plus, there's a bounty out on that Gnit guy. I could use the reward – maybe shoot him in the spine and get the kids a new sled. I think that would really be – I just thought of another place. *(Exits.)*

PETER: *(Appearing, with pieces of grass or straw on his back.)* Jesus. I hope I never see that character again. I wonder how big the reward is. *(Brief pause.)* What a night. I made some strides, though, I think. I better go try and grab some money out of my mom's purse. Yes, sir, I've got work to do.

HELEN: *(Enters with basket of food.)* Solvay thought I might find you here. And she thought your mother might need some food.

PETER: Solvay? Where is she?

HELEN: She's waiting for me. She wanted me to drop this off.

PETER: Why didn't she come?

HELEN: This is a strange century and she's very sensitive. She didn't know where you both stood on things. But she wanted me to make you sure you didn't need anything.

PETER: Of course, right, strange century, sensitivity. Tell her thank you. I don't need anything.

HELEN: Is that the truth?

PETER: *(Looking at her intently.)* Is *this* the truth?

HELEN: You look really awful – are you sick?

PETER: I haven't really been sleeping.

HELEN: Weren't you just asleep a few minutes ago?

PETER: Everyone's a comedian. *(Brief pause.)* Well, okay, so maybe not everyone.

HELEN: Is there anything else?

PETER: No. *(Brief pause.)* I think about her, a lot. I have to say. All the time, kind of. I just thought about her, last night. I felt bad. It was helpful.

HELEN: She loves you.

PETER: No, she doesn't. She loves me?

HELEN: I'm a really straightforward person.

PETER: Well then I love her. I really do. Wait! Give her this souvenir pen with the little sleigh in the snow in it. See? When you go like this he goes back and forth. Give it to her, okay?

HELEN: It's not a great gift, but, okay, I'll give it to her.

PETER: Tell her not to forget me. I have to leave again but I'll come back.

HELEN: She does love you. And she's a really good person. I don't really see what she sees in you.

PETER: How could you?

HELEN: I wish you treated people better.

PETER: Yeah. *(He takes the basket of food, looks in it, pulls out a jar of jam.)* Ohh, blueberry. Is there any – *(Rustles around through the basket.)* Ah, good. Bread. *(Looks at HELEN for a moment.)* See you later. *(HELEN exits.)*

ACT THIRD

SCENE FIRST

PETER is trying to start a chainsaw. A tree is nearby.

PETER: I'm going to cut you down, Tree. Build myself a
little mountain redoubt. Mr. Progress, coming through.
Yee-haw. *(The chainsaw doesn't start.)* Come on, *(He tries
it again.)* would you fucking start?! Goddamn it. *(Looking
off-stage.)* And on top of all that, here comes someone,
with a knife. Even my solitude isn't solitude. It's a boy, a
young man. He's stopped. My God. He just cut his finger
off. On purpose. There's a commitment. A lot of blood,
too. Now, he's walking closer. He's holding up his bleeding
hand. He's looking into my eyes, for sympathy. You got the
wrong guy, fella. He's probably a draft-dodger. Probably
trying to weasel his way out of fighting for my freedoms.
Now he's walking away, curling his little bloody hand
into his stomach. People. *(Brief pause. He fiddles with the
chainsaw.)* I should've tried it before I left the shop. *(He tries
the chainsaw one more time. It doesn't start. For just a second, he
almost starts crying.)* Goddamn this thing. Probably it just
needs to sit for a while. *(Exits.)*

SCENE SECOND

MOTHER's bedroom.

MOTHER: Explain this again.

CASE WORKER: *(She reads.)* "People v. Gnit. Insofar as the
defendant, Peter Gnit, subtitled the Unfortunate, did
knowingly and unknowingly harm and injure the plaintiff,
herefollowing delightfully denominated as The People,
and did pre-meditatively and without afterthought kidnap,
defame, or legally interrupt the normal wedding and lives
of said People, judgment is made in the amount of all

furnishings now furnishing Defendant's house, and that house itself, at an appointed time, to be appointed by – "

MOTHER: *(Interrupting.)* Thank you, okay. I think I understand.

CASE WORKER: Yeah, they're taking the house. Him threatening the judge really hurt your case. You don't seem very upset.

MOTHER: Well, I'm old.

CASE WORKER: He's off somewhere, probably drunk or asleep in a pile of leaves, without a care in the world. And look at you. You don't have anything.

MOTHER: That's not true. *(Very brief pause.)* No, I guess that's true.

CASE WORKER: Peter's going to cost you everything.

MOTHER: Something was going to cost me everything. That's how it works, isn't it? *(Brief pause.)* This is his sweater. I'm going to put some patches on the elbows.

CASE WORKER: Why don't you move into a home? A retirement place.

MOTHER: Because I already live in a home. A retirement place. And I don't have any money, dear.

CASE WORKER: I'll try to get an injunction.

MOTHER: Ooh, an injunction. Yes, you try to get that. I'll stay here with this sweater. And here's a little pen from a set that I bought for Pee-Wee. See? It has a little ship in it that goes back and forth. They won't get this. They can take my house, and my security and dignity, but they can't take my son's old sweater. Or this little thingie.

SCENE THIRD

In the woods. Birdsong. In front of PETER's new little house, which is very simple, and somewhat poorly constructed.

PETER: A house of my own, almost a home. Just a place to hang a door, really. Which is all I really need. Didn't have to deal with any realtors, either, so that was good. *(SOLVAY enters, with a suitcase.)* It's you.

SOLVAY: I know.

PETER: I can't believe it.

SOLVAY: I'm sorry.

PETER: No, my God, I'm glad.

SOLVAY: Helen said you loved me. I decided to believe her. She's really straightforward.

PETER: I do love you.

SOLVAY: I hoped so. So I left everything. I probably seem silly.

PETER: You're not silly.

SOLVAY: I know I'm not. But I probably seem it. I had a feeling. A strong simple feeling.

PETER: I've had those. God, Solvay. I'm so happy. I built this for you. You and me.

SOLVAY: I know this is strange. But let's just have faith. I know it's unbelievable, but, why can't real things be unbelievable? Leaving my father was the hardest. He said I was making a mistake, but, then he said he hoped and prayed I wasn't. That was nice. It was a lonely walk, out here. But now I'm home.

PETER: You're home. *(PETER opens the door for her, it falls off.)* We'll just put that right back on. *(He tries to put it back on. He can't, so he leans it against the house.)*

SOLVAY: Doors are hard – getting the hinges right and everything.

PETER: I know.

SOLVAY: This is such a perfect spot. Listen to the birds.

PETER: *(Listens for a moment.)* I hadn't even heard those.

SOLVAY: *(They sit for a while, enjoying the peace.)* It's getting chilly.

PETER: Go on inside, love. I'll get some wood. We'll make a little fire. *(SOLVAY goes inside. PETER walks off, begins to pick up some wood.)* Look at me, world. A calm man, with a little house and a nice person. Life, life, life: here I come.

SICK WOMAN: *(She is the WOMAN IN GREEN. Enters, incredibly aged and sick-looking, with SWADDLED BABY.)* There you are, my love.

PETER: Your "love?" Who are you? Anyway, I'm going to have to ask you and your great-grandson to excuse me.

SICK WOMAN: We were both so different, then.

PETER: When, "then"?

SICK WOMAN: When you married me.

PETER: I married you? I don't think I'd do that.

SICK WOMAN: I've been sick. I was pretty, that night. When you took me in the woods. Then I got sick.

PETER: Okay. How can I, let's see – I've done some drinking here and there, taken part in some ceremonies I probably shouldn't have, but, please, no offense, but, I'd remember you.

SICK WOMAN: We were married in a tree. You were drunk.

PETER: Good one. "We were married in a tree." See you later.

SICK WOMAN: My family's in realty. We offered you a job. You're still wearing the suit we gave you.

PETER: *(PETER remembers immediately.)* This? No, I think I got this at a…. Realty, you said? I can't, um, that's not ringing any bells. *(Brief pause.)* Sorry, I have to take a stand here. You're going to just have to leave me alone.

SICK WOMAN: I'm not going to leave you alone. *(She tends to the SWADDLED BABY.)* How do you like your little boy? I think he gets his sleep schedule from his father.

PETER: Father? How could that be? *(To himself.)* It was only, like, thirty-eight to forty weeks ago, and… Listen, um… *(He looks into the house, toward SOLVAY, then at SICK WOMAN and*

SWADDLED BABY.) Solvay? Wait for me. Please wait for me. *(He runs into the woods.)*

SICK WOMAN: If I were a witch, I'd make him get sick and old, like me, overnight. But I'm not. So I'll let him get sick and old like everyone else, in real time. So that it takes the rest of his life. It'll break his heart more, that way. It'll be more of a surprise. *(She exits.)*

SOLVAY comes out of the little house. Lights fade.

SCENE FOURTH

MOTHER's room. Door and windows are missing. MOTHER lies in a corner, very sick, wrapped in a tattered blanket. She is alone in the room, save for a dead cat lying in the middle of the floor. PETER's sweater, mended, sits neatly folded on the floor.

MOTHER: I think I hear snow. This was always a good blanket. You were always good to me. We thought we'd lost you, bankie. Everything went so fast. Is that a bunny, over there? This air can't be good for my breathing. Good riddance, all of it. My son was a good boy. What's-his-name loved me. Was I too strict? I wasn't strict. I was lonely. I wish I could cry, silly old person. Or walk in the sun along some nice canal with a pretty granddaughter. Instead of sitting in a cold smelly room, talking to myself. Hello, bunny rabbit. Do you want a carrot?

Pause. PETER enters quietly. He smells the cat. Holding his nose, almost gagging, he carries it outside.

MOTHER: Henrik? Is that you?

PETER: It's me, mom. Pee-Wee.

MOTHER: What are you doing?

PETER: I was just taking the cat out.

MOTHER: Good boy. It was beginning to smell.

PETER: You knew it was dead?

MOTHER: Remember this blanket?

PETER: I do, yeah.

MOTHER: Where have you been?

PETER: I was out kind of perfecting my –

MOTHER: *(Interrupting, quietly.)* I don't care, sweetie. *(Brief pause.)* I'm freezing, son. You ruined that wedding and then left that girl. That was stupid, dear. They sued me. They're supposed to take the house, but they said because they're Christians, they'd just take the windows and door, for now. I never imagined I'd go blind. *(Brief pause.)* How does my hair look?

PETER: It looks nice, mom.

MOTHER: I haven't washed it. I must look awful.

PETER: You look pretty.

MOTHER: Liar. *(She smiles.)* I'm glad you're here. *(Brief pause.)* I'm scared.

PETER: Don't be scared.

MOTHER: Don't tell me what not to be. You don't know anything, Peter. I love you but you don't know anything. *(Very brief pause.)* I never used to think about my eyes, when I was watching you try to grow up.

PETER: I'm sorry, mom.

MOTHER: You were searching for yourself from when you were very little. You used to ask, "Who am I?" And I would say, "You're very little." I told you crazy fairy tales. Maybe that was wrong. I tried, with you, Peter. I tried to do a good job loving you.

PETER: You were a great mother.

MOTHER: I *am* a great mother.

PETER: You *are* a great mother.

MOTHER: Not anymore. Tell me a story.

PETER: About what?

MOTHER: About this, Peter. My reality here, about which you know nothing. Make something up.

PETER: Once, in a kingdom–

MOTHER: *(Interrupting.)* No kingdoms, Peter. Don't make anything up.

PETER: Once, in a cold little room –

MOTHER: Good.

PETER: – a boy stood before his mother.

MOTHER: His *dying* mother.

PETER: His dying mother. Not knowing what to say or where to look. The boy was hardly a boy anymore. He was getting old too. He'd never really found his way into life. Yes, he had some history, he'd met a few women in his –

MOTHER: *(Interrupting.)* Keep it on the mother.

PETER: The mother held onto her blanket, and her hair looked nice, and she looked calm.

MOTHER: But she wasn't.

PETER: But she wasn't. She was afraid. She didn't know what was next.

MOTHER: She was afraid.

PETER: Her boy could see this. *(Brief pause.)* There is a limit to the magic powers of language.

MOTHER: A limit.

PETER: And they both knew, she more than he, what was coming next. Or, no, they didn't know.

MOTHER: Wait. *(She suffers, without making a sound, through a momentary pain.)* I'm sorry. *(Brief pause.)* Keep going. Go ahead, sweetie.

PETER: She knew. That there would be no kingdom. And no king. And no stories, left. *(She winces, again.)* There would be no gates, no calm, no bright light. The body knows what to do. *(PETER is having trouble breathing, perhaps crying or trying not to cry.)* The magic act of the body was over. There wouldn't be any more magic. But, there had been, before. The mother sang beautifully. She had beautiful eyes and looked out for her son. She could see. The world was magic. The boy loved his mother. The boy loved his mother.

MOTHER: He's a good boy. Keep going. Don't lie.

PETER: I won't, mom. So. Whatever it all was, it was all about to end. And the boy who was no longer a boy looked into the eyes of the mother who could no longer see. She breathed with difficulty.

MOTHER: *(Breathing with difficulty.)* Yes. It was hard for her to breathe. And him?

PETER: He breathed with difficulty. *(Brief pause.)* And so – unknowing as ever as to how to comfort the woman who had given him nothing but comfort for every day of her life, and his life, for the whole uncomfortable time – the boy who might never be a man stared at his shoes.

MOTHER: Did he hold her hand? *(PETER is not holding her hand, and, will not be.)*

PETER: He did. Tightly.

MOTHER: Good boy. Did she smile?

PETER: She did. She looked beautiful. She looked ready.

MOTHER: That's nice, dear. No, she didn't.

PETER: Didn't what? Just let me tell the story, Mom. Mom? *(Brief pause. Quietly.)* Mom? *(MOTHER has died. PETER looks out the window. Takes a deep breath. He closes her eyes with his fingers.)* This is what people do.

CASE WORKER: *(Enters.)* She was wondering if you'd make it. How is she?

PETER: And, just like that, someone walks in.

CASE WORKER: *(Realizing what's happened.)* Oh, no. I had a feeling, so I came right over.

PETER: This is one of those momentous things. *(Brief pause.)* There's a family plot. I don't know where it is or if it has to be paid for, or, if you just.... I'm sorry, I have to go.

CASE WORKER: Now? Where are you going? You're not even going to –

PETER: *(Interrupting.)* Not even going to what? *(Brief pause.)* I'm sorry. Thank you. For looking after her. She and I... Mom and I, um.... What do you say? A person says what? *(To no one in particular.)* Thank you. *(Walking out the door.)* Bye, mom.

Intermission.

ACT FOURTH

SCENE FIRST

A seaside bar in Morocco. PETER, well-dressed, much older, is holding a leather travel bag, standing at the bar, while a BARTENDER is cleaning glasses. A German, an Englishman, and a Russian, all played by INTERNATIONAL MAN, sit a table nearby.

BARTENDER: How you doing, buddy – what's new?

PETER: *(Fairly quickly, throughout. Perhaps occasionally chewing on a swizzle stick.)* Oh, Jesus, let's see. Went to a wedding a bunch of years ago, met this great woman Solvay, then ran off with the bride but changed my mind, and I had to leave town and these people sued my mother, and then I got lost and had a run-in with these crazy people – realtors, I guess – impregnated one, supposedly, then met up with something called "the middle," that was challenging, then built a little house, got back together with the great woman from the wedding, but the realtoress – who turned out to be a magical witch or had gotten sick or something – came around with my so-called son, and that ruined that, so then I had to leave again. These last few years, on the look-out for my true self, I got into the baby trade, sold plots of fake land, formed a little church, a strictly paper-based sort of thing, got very wealthy, met some more women, had a string of really successful relationships. Before that, mom went blind and died, that was hard. She was an angel, in retrospect. I left before the funeral, I don't know why, it was a confusing time – I trust she got buried all right. We always do, eventually. Then I did some more shit, tried to make some people pay for my mother's death and my dad's life, ugly stuff, nothing you'd really put on the resumé. Anyway, now I'm here: Sunny Morocco! I'm hoping to get into some arms dealing, some really serious money, as I'd like to be even richer, as I've got this massive inferiority-complex, or, this tiny superiority-complex.

46

I'm standing here right now, with my life in a bag, all my money in a bag, no reason to look back, nothing to look back at. I'm staring at you, and, I want to be the fucking Emperor. Your fucking Emperor.

BARTENDER: *(Shaking his head, smiling, agreeing, hasn't been listening.)* Women. What can I get you?

PETER: *(Brief pause.)* Did you hear one word I just said?

BARTENDER: *(Agreeing.)* Oh, man. What'll it be?

PETER: Two scotches.

INTERNATIONAL MAN: Four!

PETER: Oh, yeah – four.

INTERNATIONAL MAN: Thank you.

BARTENDER: Coming right up. *(He serves PETER the drinks. PETER returns to table with drinks.)*

INTERNATIONAL MAN: Jolly good.

PETER: Not at all.

INTERNATIONAL MAN: Danke.

PETER: It's nothing.

INTERNATIONAL MAN: Spasibo.

PETER: Okay.

INTERNATIONAL MAN: Ah, drinks. Wonderful drinks. Yes.

PETER: Let us talk about the nature of the self.

INTERNATIONAL MAN: Yum.

PETER: My single rule: "By yourself." Just do it all by yourself. A terrible man once told me that. He might not have even been human. Weird, I got my life lesson from him, but, I did, and it's stood me in good stead. Yes, a little money doesn't hurt. *(He pats his bag, which is sitting next to him.)* Nor does a lot. But, for me, personally, selfhood was always the thing. The goal. "The Self."

INTERNATIONAL MAN: That takes discipline. Discipline! And one needs a little garden in which to sit, remark the flowers, enjoy a spot of tea. I enjoy to sit in the sauna. It's so hot, in there. I think it also requires – and this will seem like a bit of a strange word choice, but – sympathy. Ja, this is correct, mein friend. We find ourselves in other people's hearts. *(Russian man is perhaps imitating English man.)* "We find ourselves in other people's hearts." Well, it's true, old man. Okay.

PETER: Well, we all have our ways. You're wonderful company, by the way. You remind me of someone. I don't care who. But I like the way you people think. Let me get another round. *(PETER is getting drunk. He gets up to get more drinks, only hearing the first three sentences.)*

INTERNATIONAL MAN: Three cheers for you. Ja. Get me some ice, will you? *(PETER is out of earshot.)* We should take this idiot's money. We should. To teach him a lesson about the value of things. And, to take his money. He is shrewd, very shrewd. We'll have to be sly as the fox, though. We must be calculating, our strategy will have to be near-perfect, to outsmart him and get his money. I have a plan. *(Whispers.)*

PETER: *(Returning with more drinks, drunker.)* So, as I was saying, I made the great refusals, suffered the lonely nights and mornings, forever in search of this *(Pointing to his chest.)*, the inside, the unvarnished mess, the thing that will die, the thing that quivers at the question "What is the thing that dies?" Yeah. I played jai alai once. Worked in finance, sort of. I met this Swiss girl, she did ballet or some kind of dancing – wow.

INTERNATIONAL MAN: *(He grabs PETER's bag, and runs off.)*

PETER: Hey, whoa! Where's the fire? *(Brief pause. To BARTENDER.)* Anyway, I slept in my shoes many many nights. God, the smell. But, you know, there was learning there. Philosophy. The self. Plus, I got rich. Here are my real friends, here. *(He goes to pat his bag, which is gone.)* Damn it. Fuck. *(He gets up.)* Who were those guys who just left?

BARTENDER: Ah, those guys. Hey, we're closing pretty soon. You don't have to go home, but, you can't stay here. "Laimigu celu," as they say in, um – Latvia, I think. Right? Latvia. Whooo, long day. It's been a long day. *(BARTENDER turns lights off, exits.)*

SCENE SECOND

INTERNATIONAL MAN enters dark stage, with PETER's bag. ROBBER appears, with a gun.

ROBBER: Give me the bag.

INTERNATIONAL MAN: Kill these two and take the money. No, kill those two. Bloody coward. "Bloody coward." Please, there's no money in here – it's just shells, some interesting rocks and shells I found. Please. These hands are lethal weap –

ROBBER: *(Interrupting. Three gun shots. INTERNATIONAL MAN is dead. ROBBER rifles through bag.)* Look at all this. I'm rich! *(Pulls out an old photograph.)* And here's an old picture of a little girl sitting on a small horse. She seems sad. Looks like it's hard to hold up the smile, like she's kind of bashful about having a face. Might as well describe the whole thing. There's some bergfrue growing in the background. And somebody's arm, holding the reins, cropped at the wrist. There's mountains. A cloud that looks like something very personal. I think it had just rained. It's a nice little picture. Someone wrote on the back, "Mom on a horse." It's funny, we're sons and daughters into the grave. I mean, not funny, but, you know, worth noting. *(He looks again at the photograph.)* She looks worried, even though she's smiling. I'm going to stay in a fancy hotel, tonight. I like the little soaps. No one is ever going to hear from me again. *(Exits.)*

SCENE THIRD

A woman, ANITRA, is standing somewhere, with a cigarette-girl tray, filled with maps and perhaps gum, etc. She speaks with an accent.

PETER: *(Enters. Fine clothes now ragged, exhibiting signs that this life is wearing on him. He stands to the side.)* God, I smell. I can't keep doing this. I'm making myself sick.

ANITRA: Welcome.

PETER: That's the word I was looking for. What have you here? *(He approaches her.)* I'll take one of your wonderful maps, please.

ANITRA: *(She hands him one.)* Two.

PETER: Here you go. *(He gives her two bills. Sees her name tag.)* Your name is Anitra?

ANITRA: Anitra.

PETER: That's quite a coincidence.

ANITRA: Thank you.

PETER: No, I mean, I knew someone with that name. It's quite a story. Unbelievable story, really.

ANITRA: Yes. Not believe story.

PETER: Maybe we could go somewhere and I could tell it to you.

ANITRA: Yes. *(She doesn't move.)* English?

PETER: What, who me? No, no. Oh, but I do *speak* English.

ANITRA: Hey, sailboat.

PETER: Hey. The thing is, Anitra, I've been going around and around the world. I got robbed, lost everything. Just had a little moment of doubt back there, but, I think I'm getting closer. I'm almost there. To the real world, the world inside. I'm different from the old me.

ANITRA: The old you.

PETER: Right. Then, sometimes, I wonder. I worry. I don't know how a person is supposed to make it all the way to his death.

ANITRA: He will be fine. He feels he is robbed. You are the old you. You don't know how.

PETER: You're very beautiful.

ANITRA: From your perspective, yes. But try to see these things like I see these things – with you standing there, next to me, so ugly inside you. In this picture, I become less attractive.

PETER: Well, I lost my luggage.

ANITRA: I just said something smart.

PETER: Yes, you've certainly got a philosophical bent.

ANITRA: I am a journalist. Enjoy some of my journalism. Thank you. *(She reads from a note pad.)* The house –

PETER: *(Interrupting.)* Your house? Do you live near here?

ANITRA: *(Brief pause.)* The house is black. The horse is breathing. The sea is water. The man is yelling. The tree is great. The life is true. This is English. Honesty is policy.

PETER: It's very good. You speak very well. *(He puts his hand on hers.)* If you like, I could give you –

ANITRA: *(Interrupting.)* Thank you so much for never touching me. That's really great. My family is waiting. I am off. Try to never imagine me. I am grateful. I am closed. *(She begins leaving.)*

PETER: No, come on, don't close. Come back.

ANITRA: What part of every word I know don't you understand? *(Exits.)*

PETER: *(Pause. He looks at the map.)* Egypt!? We're in Egypt?

SCENE FOURTH

PETER's hut. SOLVAY, much older, is sitting with PASTOR. She is working on some knitting.

PASTOR: It's coming along.

SOLVAY: I have to undo all this, I counted wrong, so, it isn't really. But I'll get it right. This is what my life is, I've decided. Sunshine, nighttime, watching the horizon, learning to knit. Oh, and eating, cooking. Sleeping. Dreaming and thinking. I guess there's a lot.

PASTOR: And of course God.

SOLVAY: Of course? I don't know about that. *(A bird sings. SOLVAY listens.)* Birds sing. I thought that, the other day, and I almost fell over. Birds sit on branches, and sing. It's just almost too much. That was a grackle, I think, or a starling. Either way, it doesn't care. It doesn't know what its name is, and it's doing just fine. I like my life.

PASTOR: I like my life too.

SOLVAY: I'm not trying to compete with you. *(She holds up some yarn.)* Is this gray?

PASTOR: Yeah, that's gray. How come I don't ever see you in church?

SOLVAY: Because I never go. Dark gray?

PASTOR: It's fairly dark. The funniest thing happened on the way over here.

SOLVAY: *(Small laugh. Supportively.)* That's so funny. *(Brief pause.)* I'm sorry, I'm in sort of a solitary mood. But I'm glad you're here.

PASTOR: Of course. You should come. To church.

SOLVAY: Why?

PASTOR: Salvation.

SOLVAY: Oh. Maybe I already have that. But I guess it's not for me to say. Or you, either. *(Holding up the knitting to look at it.)* My eyes aren't very good. I've always thought you were very nice.

PASTOR: Thank you.

SOLVAY: You're welcome. Pastor, did you know, I used to be a girl.

PASTOR: Of course. Everyone was a girl. I mean, all females.

SOLVAY: You're a very wise man. *(Brief pause, knitting.)* This is my life. *(Birdsong, sparrow.)* That was a sparrow.

SCENE FIFTH

In the vicinity of the SPHINX.

PETER: Now, *(He looks at his map.)* seriously, where are we, exactly?

SPHINX: *(Voice, off-stage.)* This.

PETER: Who said that? What?

SPHINX: Nothing. I just said: This.

PETER: Oh, Jesus, are you like that other thing?

SPHINX: Yes. *(Very brief pause.)* What other thing?

PETER: The middle.

SPHINX: Yes. And I have a riddle for you to solve. Solve it or Die. What goes "Tap, Tap, Pause, Pause, Tap" – you know what, actually? – forget that, forget about that. Instead, tell me, have you learned anything since last we met?

PETER: I am continuing to explore the self.

SPHINX: So that's a "no"?

PETER: I have to ask again, who are you?

SPHINX: Who are you? *(Voice of BEGRIFFIN, doing a gentle echo.)* Wer bist du? Wer bist du? Wer bist du?

PETER: That's crazy. The echo echoes back in German. Seriously, hello? Who are you?

SPHINX: Why do you think you're so special?

53

PETER: I don't. I mean, I do, but, you know.

SPHINX: The truth is outside.

PETER: Interesting. But, no, just explain to me what –

SPHINX: *(Interrupting.)* And, suddenly, strangely, but logically, but oddly, and sadly, but truly, I'm gone.

A German-looking man appears from behind the Sphinx.

PETER: Jesus. I thought I was alone.

BEGRIFFIN: Guten tag. Sorry – I mean, Good day. I was doing the German echo.

PETER: *(Little laugh.)* So that's what that was. You had me wondering.

BEGRIFFIN: Did I. Begriffin.

PETER: Sorry?

BEGRIFFIN: Is the name. Begriffin. Touring around, are you? On holiday, are we? Just having fun, is he?

PETER: Are you just one person?

BEGRIFFIN: Yes.

PETER: I thought so. Can't hurt to ask, right?

BEGRIFFIN: Oh, it can hurt. But, go on.

PETER: Well, okay, so, I'm visiting all those places in the world that remain, like myself, great mysteries. I've wanted to solve the mystery of the Sphinx all my life.

BEGRIFFIN: Und? Excuse me – and?

PETER: It's only a mystery because it's perceived by a mystery. But we are not neutral, we are not un-mysterious. So it takes on shadows. Look on it and gaze upon the strange and crumbling statue inside yourself.

BEGRIFFIN: Okay. *(He stares at the statue.)* Not bad. But, this is interesting. You think the Sphinx is you.

PETER: I can only claim this as I am, first and last-most, myself. The only actual person I know.

BEGRIFFIN: Are you.

PETER: I want to be the Emperor. Bring back the Empire, and, be its Emperor.

BEGRIFFIN: Tell me, would you like to speak to some people? I'm the director of a – I don't know what the word would be – area? Let's call it an area. I think the – what would be the word? People? Let's call them people – I think the people there might appreciate your theory.

PETER: Really?

BEGRIFFIN: Ja. Sorry, again – yeah.

PETER: A think-tank, is it, you say? Well, I'm very flattered. You mean luncheons and dinners, that kind of thing? I do have some experience. So, absolutely. Of course I will be the new artist-in-residence of your research center.

BEGRIFFIN: It's really more of an area. A place where they stay.

PETER: Finally. Someone who sees me for what I am.

SCENE SIXTH

They walk across the stage, enter a high-security building. PETER sees it for some sort of research institute. SHACKLETON is standing against a wall. DARK LADY is there.

BEGRIFFIN: I'll be right back. Have a look around.

PETER: *(To SHACKLETON.)* Hello, sir. Dr. Peter Gnit. Enchanted.

SHACKLETON: Also enchanted. Totally enchanted, now that I think of it.

PETER: What's your specialty?

SHACKLETON: Oh I think they're all pretty good.

PETER: I think I would agree.

SHACKLETON: Say that again. I can't hear out of this ear. And I wasn't paying attention.

DARK LADY: *(Shaking her head.)* Women. I mean, men. No, I was right the first time. Watch out for me. Just a thought.

PETER: Yes. Interesting group. *(Very brief pause.)* Now, I'm looking around for a podium. And perhaps some bottled water. Will it be held in here? And, when do we begin?

DARK LADY: Ahem. Yes, you heard right – a female can say "ahem." So. The world is two-thirds water, one-half women, leaving men the last little rest. The world is one-sixth men. I used math to come to my conclusion. Fractions, if I have to come right out and say it.

SHACKLETON: *(Trying to free himself, revealing that he is chained to the wall in shackles.)* Agh, these things are *(He squirms, a little.)*, God, it's just really hard to move around.

PETER: Oh, no. You're – is this part of an experiment?

SHACKLETON: Yeah, I guess.

DARK LADY: People seem to enjoy what I have to say. Or, they *would.*

PETER: So, you're all – it's my understanding – you're all investigating the Self? *(Brief pause, as no one responds or says anything.)* I've been invited here to speak.

DARK LADY: *(Pause.)* So why isn't he saying anything?

SHACKLETON: *(To PETER.)* But, seriously, very nice to meet you. I'm in Men's Clothing. What do you do?

PETER: As I said, I'm here to give a lecture on a subject of some mystery. Me. This, along with a theory of mine that I think some people will find very interesting.

DARK LADY: Hey, when's lunch?

SHACKLETON: I know, I'm starving.

BREMER: *(Enters, pushed in by an unseen hand.)* Hi. *(Brief pause.)* I just got here.

PETER: Yes. Hello. Me too.

BREMER: No time for niceties.

PETER: No, of course. Are you also speaking today?

BREMER: I was just speaking five seconds ago.

DARK LADY: He was. Probably closer to ten seconds, now.

PETER: No, I mean, are you, like myself, going to expound on a subject in which you're an expert?

BREMER: *(Very brief pause.)* Don't ever change. Hand me that pencil, would you. *(PETER hands the pencil to BREMER.)*

SHACKLETON: What's your speech about, again? Me?

PETER: No. Me. *(Trying to ignore all the disturbing signs.)* Where did the gentleman go? Begriffin, is it? I'm not sure that this is –

BREMER: *(Interrupting. He sticks the pencil in his eye.)* Ah, fuck – my eye. I've made a terrible mistake. But, you know, I learned something. Now what's my next step here.

PETER: *(In horror.)* Oh, God.

SHACKLETON: I wanted to stop him. Part of me did. The rest of me thought: no, let's just see where this is going. *(To PETER.)* You were right next to him.

DARK LADY: It's true. Either you ignored your instincts, or your instincts were wrong, or, you don't have any instincts. And that's just three things.

BEGRIFFIN: *(Enters.)* Oh, Jeez. Medic! *(He shuttles BREMER out the door.)* There we are. Have you met everyone?

PETER: What is this place? I don't think – . I'm not sure that I should really –

BEGRIFFIN: *(Interrupting.)* Nonsense – you're just filled with fear because it's all so scary. We'll get you your washcloth. And you get a cup, in addition – make sure you put your name on it. Then you can settle in, get the feel of the place. I just did your paperwork.

PETER: My paper –

BEGRIFFIN: *(Interrupting.)* Yes. Paperwork. You're in, officially. All stamped up and stapled. *(Sounds of medic screaming, off-stage.)* I think we can help.

PETER: Help? Help what?

BEGRIFFIN: You.

PETER: I don't need help. These people need help. I'm just myself. My true self.

BEGRIFFIN: So are they. They're nothing but themselves. All reason, no sympathy. Hi, everyone. You can be their Emperor. Some of your ideas would make a nice little footnote in an article I want to write. This is great. You'll be fine, here. Feeding is at seven. Excuse. *(Exits.)*

SHACKLETON: He's serious – make sure you put your name on your cup. I never did and someone took mine. You're thinking, "Mister, you must be thirsty." I'm thinking, "Mister, I really am."

DARK LADY: Collective nouns. You know? *(Brief pause.)* I have theories. *(To PETER.)* You do look scared. Deep down. What was your name, again? No, wait, let me guess. *(Pause.)* You know what, I don't want to guess your name.

BREMER: *(Enters, pushed into the room.)* That medic needs a medic. *(To PETER.)* Could you hand me that other pencil?

PETER: I'm not supposed to be here. I'm a sane person.

BREMER: I need that pencil, yesterday. I mean, today.

PETER: I have to get out of here. How do I get out of here?

A low rumble.

SHACKLETON: That's an earthquake. I can sense these things. Not to be negative, but, I think it's going to get worse. *(The rumble becomes almost deafening. A section of wall collapses. All is very quiet.)*

DARK LADY: *(Pause.)* It's so quiet. Did you see me shaking, just then?

PETER runs off, through the hole in the wall.

DARK LADY: Typical. *(She and BREMER drift off. SHACKLETON is still handcuffed to a section of wall.)*

SHACKLETON: *(Brief pause. A fire has quietly started.)* Huh. That's a pretty good fire going there. *(Very brief pause.)* I wish I were the type to write memoirs. History never really hears from people like me. *(Very brief pause.)* But anyway,

here I am. It's weird. It's a big world. So many different
people – high and low, weak and strong, dying presidents
and little girls with eyeglasses. Where does a guy like
me, chained up in a burning building, fit in? What's an
important human being? You know? How do you be
good, in life, on earth? At least I never really hurt anyone.
That's sort of a comfort. But not for you. *(Lights fade as he is
consumed by the flames.)*

ACT FIFTH

SCENE FIRST

Home. A sign announces "Arrivals." Another sign says "Welcome. Willkommen. Bienvenue. Benvenuto. Maligayang pagdating." PETER enters, older still, carrying a bag, passing under the Arrivals sign. BEGGAR, one-legged, is dressed in rags and sitting on the ground, with a paper cup before him.

PETER: Ah. And so, after all the years, all the other times and places I stood and said, "Here I am," I now stand here, now, and say – .

BEGGAR: *(Interrupting.)* Help. Please. Thank you.

PETER: Don't get up, don't get up – I prefer this arrangement. Help is on the way. *(He is reaching into his luggage.)* In fact, I owe a stranger a favor or two. I just had some lucky years. So, guess what, I want you to have half of what I have. Why not. I'm feeling just that grateful. Just that happy to be home. *(He begins opening the large bag.)*

A PALE MAN in a dark suit enters, crosses upstage, lingers.

BEGGAR: You're too good, sir.

PETER: I know, I know. *(Glances at PALE MAN.)*

BEGGAR: This is too kind. You're a good person.

PETER: No, no – I understand life. I understand living. *(To PALE MAN.)* Yes?

PALE MAN: Are you, by any chance, an organ donor?

PETER: Excuse me?

PALE MAN: Nothing. *(He mumbles a sentence, the only audible part of which is the words "Kierkegaardian Dread.")*

PETER: What?

PALE MAN: You have nice eyes.

PETER: I'm sorry?

PALE MAN: Oh, yeah? Bye, now. *(Exits.)*

BEGGAR: What did he say, in the middle? Kiergegaardian *what?* That was weird. But, I can't tell you how much this means. My family will be so happy.

PETER: *(Brief pause. Still slightly preoccupied with PALE MAN, but only for a moment more.)* Right. Family. Family meaning mother and father? Some brothers, a sister?

BEGGAR: Children. Two daughters, sir. And a wonderful wife who deserves more.

PETER: Ah. I see. *(Brief pause.)* Take us through the scene. When you walk through the door, with your new-found riches, which are half of my hard-fought gains.

BEGGAR: Ah, okay – happily. Probably the dog greets me, wiggling and ducking into me. The children run to my side. My wife smiles, sees what I have, she starts to cry. We stand together in our little room, crying and laughing and praising your name, with the dog, wagging, jumping up. The happiest house in the world. In the evening, after a filling meal, before the fire, we'll sit together and plan tomorrow. Maybe a boat ride. We all cuddle together, feeling sleepy and safe. There's a beautiful glow. A glow that never fully went away, even in the hardest times. And now it's blazing. Love and hope, sir. Love and hope are blazing.

PETER: What'd you have children for? Knowing you couldn't provide for them.

BEGGAR: Oh, I could provide, sir. And did. *(Raises his stump of a leg.)* Then I lost this, in a machine. I hear my family's stomachs growl, at night. And in the morning. So I sit out here, on the ground, looking up at everyone, asking for help. Just until I find something else. *(He laughs, humbly.)* Something I can still do.

PETER: I see. Tell you what, Dad – I changed my mind. This is probably going to sound harsh, but, fuck you and fuck your family's growling stomachs. Ooooh. It sounds so much worse when you say it out loud. *(PETER looks at his watch, looks off.)*

BEGGAR: I don't think I... You're not going to help me?

PETER: Is there still a steakhouse down this way? Ah, how would you know. *(Very brief pause.)* I think we're done here. Unless you can think of anything you wanted to add? Great. *(Exits.)*

BEGGAR: Mankind. *(Brief pause. He is trying not to cry, mainly succeeding.)* I can't even tell anyone about this.

SCENE SECOND

A graveyard, a funeral in progress. Mourners gathered around. GRAVEDIGGER waits, to the side. PETER saunters by, with a linen napkin tucked into the opening of his shirt. He stands nearby, listening.

PASTOR: In death, the hearing is one of the first things to go. So this eulogy is mainly meant for you, the still-living, the still-hearing. We all knew the recently departed as Gimp. But there was more to him. *(PETER saunters nearby.)* Hey, great – hello, hello. Didn't know people still cared. Anyway, the first time I saw Gimp was while I was a member of the local Draft Board. You all remember how he cut off his finger, because he didn't want to fight. He believed in peace. On that day, as he left Town Hall, everyone threw trash at him and called him a traitor, and he ran for the hills. There, he started a small ski resort. He married his childhood sweetheart, had three beautiful boys. An avalanche destroyed the ski resort and he rebuilt it as an emu ranch, which went broke. The boys moved away and the childhood sweetheart died, as childhood sweethearts do. Gimpy came to church, from time to time. And he came with humility. Not shame, but humility. He could have made like Job, made a big stink about his terrible luck. He didn't. He took up gardening, instead. He grew beets, which were delicious. I have a weakness, some of you know, for beet salad – some bleu cheese, some balsamic vinaigrette – right, Nancy? Is Nancy here? The

point is, he tried. That's a life. Trying, and, loving. That is a
real life. He now stands before his God, intact, resplendent.
Imagine that, standing before God, and being proud of
yourself, quietly and humbly proud of yourself. I think
that's what God wants. If there is a god. And I think there
probably is. Anyway, please stop by the house for coffee
and pie and we'll keep saying bye-bye deep into the night.
Let us go in peace. *(PASTOR and MOURNERS exit.)*

PETER: Let us go however we want. *(Looks into the grave.)* Was
this him, all those years ago, the boy I saw cut his finger
off? Kindred spirit. Both of us: ourselves. He at least had a
family who turned against him or died. I don't even have
a skull to talk to. *(Brief pause.)* I wonder if I was too hard
on that beggar. Nah. Beggars are beggars for a reason. And
he's got his wife and kids. *(He looks into the grave again.)*

GRAVEDIGGER: *(Enters, with a shovel. Quietly, hoarsely.)* Show
time.

PETER: Hi. *(Watches him dig for a while.)* You've seen some
things in your day, I imagine. All the weeping and gritted
teeth. It must give a man a certain perspective, looking at
life like that.

GRAVEDIGGER: *(Hoarsely.)* I have laryngitis. Sorry. I shouldn't
talk.

PETER: No, of course. You know, I knew him. Not well, but, I
knew him. You might say that he and I were –

GRAVEDIGGER: *(Interrupting sharply, same as above, but a little
louder.)* I have laryngitis.

PETER: Right, okay. Take care of that.

GRAVEDIGGER: Oh, I will. I need some more dirt. *(Exits.)*

PALE MAN: *(Enters.)* Remember me?

PETER: Yeah, just from a few hours ago, I think I –

PALE MAN: *(Interrupting.)* We have some history. Dot dot
dot dot dot. I'm hoping you'll give your body to science.
Remember? So that some good will have come of it. But
first…

PETER: *(Brief pause.)* Yes?

PALE MAN: *(Making a little gesture with his hand.)* "I'm a piece of lint!"

PETER: *(Trying to play along.)* Oh, okay. Hello, piece of lint.

PALE MAN: I'm not a piece of lint. I was testing your lack of integrity. And, good news – you passed. *(Brief pause.)* I just have to say this. *(Very quietly and plainly.)* Repent.

PETER: Excuse me?

PALE MAN: Nothing. Just, you know, an imperative. Sometimes, it's only that loud. I'll see you soon.

PETER: I don't know what this was about.

PALE MAN: I know you don't. I know. Don't worry – everything's going to be fine. *(Brief pause.)* Did I just say "everything?" And did I say "fine?" Sorry – I was thinking of something else. Well, I've to go get some milk. See you later, body. *(Exits. PETER begins to exit, has a thought, stays. Lights cross-fade.)*

SCENE THIRD

An outdoor auction. TOWN is there, with others.

AUCTIONEER: *(He pulls PETER's old sweater out of a box. He speaks calmly.)* Okay. Last item, here we go. Don't know where this stuff is from. It's a whole box, here. We have a, let's see here, a sweater. Do I hear… one dollar? Two dollars? One. For the sweater. *(TOWN nods. AUCTIONEER points.)* Okay, I've got one right here. Now, let's really get it going. Looking for two dollars. For the sweater.

PASTOR: Is it wool?

AUCTIONEER: Is it wool. *(He looks for a label.)* You know, I don't know, it doesn't say. Handmade, so there's no label. It's got two nice patches. Somebody really loved somebody. A good heavy sweater. Might be a blend. Couple of stains. Probably tears, right? But, seriously, here we go, for one dollar. Going once. Going twice. Sold. Right

here. One dollar. *(TOWN hands over a bill, takes sweater.)*
Now… let's see. *(Looking into the box.)* We have some more
stuff in here, and then we're done. All junk, looks to be.
A novelty pen, an old cat collar, and some other stuff.
The things people save. A dollar for the box. Do I hear a
dollar? I do not. Going, going, gone.

TOWN: Nobody bid anything.

AUCTIONEER: I know. *(AUCTIONEER puts the box in a trash can.)*

TOWN: Can I have that?

AUCTIONEER: Yeah, I don't care. *(TOWN gets the box from the
trash.)* Next week, we have some interesting stuff. *(He
refers to a piece of paper.)* Let's see here, *(Reading.)* "Blank
gravestones, a tandem bicycle, paper." A lot of paper,
in fact – I think it's from a stationery store that closed or
moved. See you then.

*AUCTIONEER exits. PETER enters. PALE MAN walks by, opposite
direction as he last exited, carrying a bottle of milk.*

PALE MAN: Milk. Good for the bones and teeth. *(He exits.)*

PETER: *(REPORTER, wearing a sweater, enters, with a camera, a
notepad.)* Who was that, do you know? That just walked
by?

REPORTER: Him? The guy with the milk? I did a feature on
him, once. He runs sort of a medical clinic, here. His son-
in-law killed himself – Moynihan was the name. Then his
daughter died. He had some really dark years, lot of anger
about everything, but then he, you know, I don't know,
he changed. He got into suicide prevention and started a
hospice. He delivered both my kids. Good guy. Weird, but,
good guy.

PETER: Well, the world needs doctors.

REPORTER: Yeah. Yes it does.

PETER: You were saying, you did a feature?

REPORTER: I do a column. It's called "Total Individuals."

PETER: Well, I can see why you've approached me.

REPORTER: Didn't approach, just was walking by.

PETER: I am, yes, how shall I say it, something of an individual. Total? That'll be for the reader to decide. But I suppose I am, drum roll...myself.

REPORTER: Okay. Drum roll...how so?

PETER: Well, I've travelled around the world. Seven seas, all that.

REPORTER: Yeah, that's great. I love traveling.

PETER: Ah, yes, but I was always traveling in pursuit of myself. I always marched to the beat of my own drum.

REPORTER: Yeah, nice. I guess my thing, my column, it's more devoted to people who kind of used their selves to pursue Some Other Thing, you know?

PETER: You're not getting me.

REPORTER: Mmmh, no, I think I get you. And I think it's great you weren't tied down and you did a lot of going around.

PETER: It was more than that.

REPORTER: Yeah, you said.

PETER: My name – I guess for some legal reason you need me to officially say it – my name is Peter Gnit.

REPORTER: Okay. *(He writes it down.)* "Peter Gnit. Travel buff."

PETER: No. "Peter Gnit. Self. Actual Self." *(Brief pause.)* I said it was more than traveling. I overcame things. I came from nothing. My slogan was, "By yourself."

REPORTER: Everyone has a self. It's great you have one, but, you know, so does everyone. *(Brief pause.)* It's funny, I think "By Yourself" was an old advertising slogan for a real estate agency. They were trying to encourage home-ownership.

PETER: What?

REPORTER: Yeah. They got shut down, I'm pretty sure.

PETER: *(Very brief pause.)* I went to America.

REPORTER: Beautiful country.

PETER: I saw the Sphinx.

REPORTER: Wow! You've really done all the cruises and stuff. You know, we do another little feature, kind of a fun thing, called, "They Eat *What*?" It's about exotic foods from different countries. I bet you've eaten some of those.

PETER: I've suffered. I've made myself suffer, all my life. We are talking about my soul. About the achievements of my soul on Earth.

REPORTER: It comes out every other week. *(Brief pause.)* I'm sorry.

PETER: I'm sort of panicking and drawing a blank. There's more to me than what I'm saying.

REPORTER: Hey, no, come on. I would love to see the Sphinx, you know? *(Brief pause.)* What brought you back around here, anyway?

PETER: Love? A woman I loved. I still love.

REPORTER: Oh yeah?

PETER: I haven't seen her in thirty years. I don't know if she's still here, or if she's married or even still alive.

REPORTER: Now that could be something. "Lovers reunited after thirty years." That really would be interesting. *(Hands him a business card.)* I mean, potentially. Keep me posted.

PETER: My life started on a Tuesday night, and, here it is, here I am, an old man, on Friday morning.

REPORTER: It kind of ruins the joke, when you explain it.

PETER: It's not a joke.

REPORTER: No, I know.

PETER: I've gone through my life like a person cutting through a train station to stay out of the rain.

REPORTER: Yeah, no, that's pretty good, quite the poet – wow. It does go pretty fast, doesn't it. *(Brief pause.)* I have to run. Let me know about your love story. And send us something for the food thing, okay? If you want. Although, nothing on weird bugs or whale blubber – we've already had that.

PETER: *(Brief pause.)* One time, I had a meal that was –

REPORTER: *(Interrupting.)* Sorry. Good meeting you, Mr...? I'm sorry, I forget your...wait, don't tell me. Gynt, right? See, that's the mind of the journalist, at work. Never forget a name. See you later. *(PETER stares at him, sadly. REPORTER exits. TOWN enters, carrying the box from earlier, and PETER's sweater.)*

PETER: Hi.

TOWN: Is it?

PETER: What?

TOWN: Oh. I thought you said, "Good day."

PETER: No.

TOWN: Hi.

PETER: What's in the box?

TOWN: Nothing. Details.

PETER: I remember you.

TOWN: Yeah?

PETER: *(Brief pause.)* Didn't you used to be more talkative?

TOWN: Yeah. People moved, people died. Now it's just me.

PETER: Ah. *(Brief pause.)* Do you remember Solvay?

TOWN: Of course. She went blind.

PETER: That was my mother who went blind.

TOWN: More than one person can go blind. She lives in the woods.

PETER: No. In our little house? She's still there?

TOWN: I think so.

PETER: Can you take me there?

TOWN: It's a free country.

SCENE FOURTH

They walk slowly around the stage.

TOWN: Are you all right with this pace?

PETER: I've walked these mountains all my life. *(Sound of a seagull squawking.)* What was that?

TOWN: Seagull.

PETER: How *is* Solvay? Did she ever, is she married?

TOWN: Don't know. Do you ever go like this? *(He puffs up his cheeks with air, and then blows it out in four quiet puffs.)* I do. I mean, obviously. *(Brief pause.)* Oh, this is funny. *(He points to a house.)* A couple used to live back up there. You remember them? Moynihan? He hung himself. She died later, of a broken heart and an auto-immune disorder. Of course you remember them. *(Brief pause.)* Funny is totally the wrong word. It was so sad.

PETER: That is sad.

TOWN: That's exactly what I just fucking said, verbatim. *(Brief pause.)* I think my blood sugar is really low.

PETER picks up a wild onion.

PETER: Do you know why this onion is like my life?

TOWN: I don't know, because it smells and it makes you cry? Because it's no good by itself? Because if you peel it, I don't know, you just keep peeling it, and there's nothing there except layers? Because there's no, whatever, center to it? Is that what you mean? But more importantly, here's a question for you: why would you want to stop, on your way to see a woman who's been waiting for you for thirty years, to philosophize about an onion?

PETER: That's a good... You've raised a very –

TOWN: *(Interrupting.)* You don't have to say anything.

PETER: Then I won't. *(Very brief pause.)* I know I don't have to say anything.

TOWN: Hey, little advice: ssshhh.

They continue walking, and approach the little house, on the front of which is an old torn banner that says, "Welcome Home My". Woodland birdsong is heard.

PETER: I'd forgotten what a beautiful spot this was. It was here all along. My place on Earth.

The voice of a woman is heard, singing.

TOWN: You're in luck. Sounds like she's home.

PETER: *(Moved, to tears, or almost.)* Oh God. What a beautiful sound. She waited. Solvay! I'm home!

Brief pause. ANNA steps out of the little house, with cleaning supplies.

ANNA: Solvay Breeland? I'm so sorry. Are you a relative? I was just cleaning up.

PETER: No. No she didn't.

ANNA: Can I ask who you are?

PETER: Peter.

ANNA: Peter Gnit? I recognize you from the drawings she used to do. *(Brief pause.)* I thought what you did to her was horrible. But she told me, right before the end of her life, how much she loved her life. She said she learned the genius of staying in one place, thanks to you. And how much of the world you get to see when you just stay looking for one thing. She got to be quite a bird expert.

PETER: *(Close to devastated. Almost without affect.)* I don't think I can – . *(Brief pause.)* It's too late, but now I'm home. Solvay, darling, I'm still your boy inside, and I'm home.

ANNA: I don't know if you know this, but, she bought all this land.

PETER: She did? Oh my darling. She was a very smart woman.

ANNA: And she willed it to the Nature Society. As a bird sanctuary. She loved people but she said no people could live here. She loved you and said if you loved her, and you ever came back, you'd understand. People offered her a lot of money but she said no. It was just who she was.

PETER: Yes. *(Brief pause.)* I don't imagine there was any kind of a clause?

ANNA: No, it was very simple.

TOWN: When she believed a thing, she believed a thing. It's beautiful up here. They flock from all over, rare crazy birds from all over.

PETER: I don't know how to live. I never did. Not once. I don't know how to live.

ANNA: Oh. I'm sorry. *(Brief pause.)* Is it – this is going to sound awful, but – is it that hard? Other people figured it out. It's in thousands of books. It's in every religion.

TOWN: There are clubs and groups that are good, too. I think it's important to just –

PETER: *(Interrupting.)* Oh, I could have read a book, you say? Sung in a choir?

TOWN: No, no – we were just saying –

PETER: *(Interrupting.)* Could you please take pity on an old person with nothing, not one single fucking thing, and leave me alone!? *(The birdsong stops. All quiet.)*

ANNA: *(Brief pause.)* I'm sure we were only trying –

PETER: *(Interrupting.)* I don't need you to try. I need you to go away.

ANNA: Stay as long as you need. You can't stay, though. The charter is very clear about that, that nobody... *(PETER glares at her. ANNA and TOWN exit.)* We'll leave you alone for a bit.

PETER: *(A long pause. PETER looks at the little house, touches some of the woodwork.)* Solvay? Hello, sweetie. *(He listens for a moment. Quietly, to SOLVAY, and the silent birds.)* Where are your little birdies? *(PETER, in a rage, but very slowly because he's old, partly pulls down the banner, and begins to try to tear the little house down. He can't. Quietly, again.)* I can't even wreck anything right. God. *(To audience, in what should feel like the first true direct address of the play.)* You. Sympathize with me, if you're so sympathetic. Love a cruel old man who hates you, if you're so loving. I hate you. *(Very brief pause.)* I'm sorry. I'm so sorry. *(Brief pause.)* Solvay, come back. Don't leave me. *(Brief pause.)* This isn't literature. *(Brief pause.)* Mom?

TOWN: *(Pause. Enters.)* Sorry, Peter? Mr. Gnit? *(Looks at a broken window or other small sign of damage.)* Wow, look what you've done. *(Very brief pause.)* Hey, I know you were going to sit for a while, but, I haven't eaten. And I was thinking maybe you'd like to go down to the –

PETER: *(Interrupting.)* No. Forgive me. That's nice of you, but, I've eaten enough.

TOWN: Yeah? You already ate? Okay. Just thought I'd ask. *(Exits.)*

PETER: *(Out, to audience.)* My little poem is over. I'm gone. Who's next? You? You? You? You? You? *(Looking at the audience. With simple gentleness and affection.)* Ahh. Look at everyone. All dressed up and...and with your hair nice and combed. *(A rueful but not completely cold smile.)* I wish this had been happier.

He picks up a piece of lumber, then, using it as a cane, he walks upstage into the black woods. Stops and pokes at something on the ground for a moment, then walks off and disappears. A single bird begins a sparse song. Lights fade.

End.